Winnona Park
Elementary School

MOJANG

MINECRAFT™

DEL REY
NEW YORK

Published in the United States by Del Rey, an imprint of Random House, a division of Penguin Random House LLC, New York.

DEL REY and the HOUSE colophon are registered trademarks of Penguin Random House LLC.

Originally published in hardcover in the United Kingdom by Egmont UK Limited.

ISBN 978-1-101-96644-0
Ebook ISBN 978-0-525-48602-2

Printed in China on acid-free paper by RRD Asia Printing Solutions

Written by Stephanie Milton

Illustrations by Mahendra Singh
(Pages 10-13, 18-21, 26-29, 34-37, 42-53, 62-65)
Illustrations by Swampbaron
(Pages 14-17, 22-25, 30-33, 38-41, 54-61, 66-69)

randomhousebooks.com

2 4 6 8 9 7 5 3 1

First US Edition

Design by John Stuckey and Ian Pollard

CONTENTS

INTRODUCTION

When I first discovered the mysterious world of Minecraft, I set myself
an ambitious goal: to visit every biome in existence. I trekked across the
vast and colorful Overworld, ventured deep into the fiery Nether and
eventually found my way to the barren islands of the End dimension.
This book is the result of my epic journey – upon discovering each
wondrous biome, I created a highly detailed map of what I saw and
supplemented each map with observational notes and sketches.

Let me tell you a little bit about myself: I'm a loot-seeker – I live for the
moments when I discover rare treasures in new and unexpected places.
I've never enjoyed combat, however, and I'm always looking for
cunning ways to evade dangerous mobs while out exploring.

So, as I traveled through each new biome I made a note of the most significant mobs, blocks and structures I found there. This helped me to identify the biomes where I was most likely to find rare and valuable items to help me to survive, as well as the biomes where I was least likely to perish at the hands of dangerous mobs.

Now I'd like to share my findings with you. I hope that by studying this book you'll be better prepared for, and more excited about, your next expedition.

Are you ready for an adventure?

THE LOOTER

A FEW NOTES

Before we begin, there are a few terms that need to be defined. As well as understanding what a biome is, there are some other characteristics to familiarize yourself with – you'll see notes on these characteristics as we explore each biome.

BIOMES

Minecraft is divided into regions with distinct climates, geographical features, plant life and mobs – living, moving creatures. These biomes determine the shape of the terrain and its height above sea level. There are fifteen major biomes and most have a few variant types that contain slightly different features. Each biome presents unique opportunities and dangers for explorers.

Different blocks and items can be found in different biomes – sometimes exclusively. Although creepers, skeletons, zombies, spiders and endermen appear in most biomes, some mobs only spawn in one or two biomes. Whether you're looking for rare treasures or you're on the hunt for dangerous mobs, choosing the right biome for your particular goal can make the difference between success and failure. Knowledge is power!

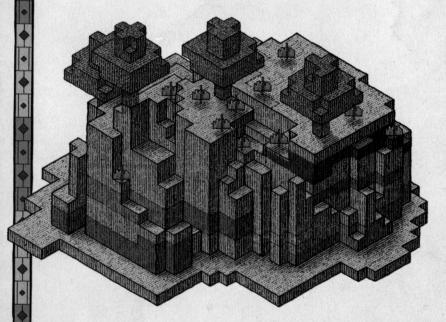

BIOME CATEGORIES

Biomes are classified into one of five categories: snowy, cold, medium/lush, dry/warm and aquatic.

In snowy biomes it snows at any altitude and the foliage and grass are dark green. In cold biomes it snows once you reach a certain altitude but rains below that point, and the foliage and grass are dark green. In medium/lush biomes it will snow at higher altitudes, otherwise it will rain, and the foliage and grass are bright green except in swamps and dark forests.

There is no precipitation at all in dry/warm biomes. The foliage and grass are more of an olive green, except in badlands biomes, where the grass is brown. Aquatic biomes are covered in water and have little or no land exposed.

TEMPERATURE

Different biomes have different temperatures, depending on their category and features. Temperature affects precipitation and the color of the grass and foliage.

It's measured on a scale from -0.5, as in the snowy taiga, to 2.0, which is the temperature in the desert.

PRECIPITATION

Rain and snow also affect the color of the grass and foliage. Where rainfall is common, the foliage tends to be a lush green. In areas where it doesn't rain, the foliage is faded and dull. Rainfall is measured on a scale from 0.0 to 1.0 and only occurs in biomes with a temperature between 0.15 and 0.95. Snow occurs in biomes with a temperature less than 0.15. No precipitation occurs in biomes with a temperature over 0.95.

ALTITUDE

Altitude measures your vertical distance within the world. It's particularly useful to know what altitude you're at when mining for ores that only generate between certain levels. The bottom of the world is 0 and everything else in the world is measured in blocks above that. Sea level is 62 blocks above the bottom of the world, clouds begin to form at level 127 and the very top of the world is 256.

VARIANTS

Most major biomes have at least one variant – a rarer type of that biome with slightly different features. The flower forest, for example, is a variant of the regular forest biome. It shares many of the same characteristics but is covered with flowers and has fewer trees.

BADLANDS

The surface of this rare biome was covered in distinctive red sand, topped with mounds of terracotta. As a loot-seeker, visiting badlands was a real treat – I discovered gold ore generating at all levels and abandoned mine shafts visible at the surface, so it was remarkably easy to find rare blocks and items. I had no desire to settle in badlands permanently, however – with no passive mobs to provide meat, I found myself getting very hungry.

GOLD ORE

LAVA POOL

TERRACOTTA

ABANDONED MINE SHAFT

CAVE SPIDER

CACTUS

LAKE

RED SAND

DEAD BUSH

OBSERVATIONS

CATEGORY: Dry/warm
TEMPERATURE: 2.0
PRECIPITATION: None
VARIANTS: Eroded badlands, badlands plateau
DANGEROUS MOBS: 8

Terracotta

The terracotta hills were a valuable source of materials for me – I've always favored terracotta as a build material, as it has the same blast resistance as stone but looks much more polished. I smelted terracotta in a furnace to produce brightly patterned blocks of glazed terracotta – these were perfect for adding decorative detail to my builds.

Abandoned Mine Shaft

Badlands was the only biome where I found an abandoned mine shaft at the surface. It was built from dark oak rather than the usual regular oak and offered me easy access to the bottom of the world, where I could mine rare ores. I also took many of the rails from inside the mine shaft, and used them to build my very own mine-cart system between biomes.

Loot Chests

Mine shafts are famous for their loot chests, and I found several sitting in mine carts throughout the tunnels. In addition to food, they also contained rare items like diamonds, rails and golden apples.

Food Sources

In the absence of passive mobs to provide meat, there weren't many sources of food here except the occasional cluster of sugar canes growing near water. Fortunately, I also found bread, melon seeds, pumpkin seeds and beetroot seeds in a loot chest in the mine shaft.

GOLD RUSH STATION BUILD

I found such vast quantities of gold ore in the badlands that I had to build somewhere to store it all. I looted dark oak planks from the mine shaft and constructed a gold rush station at the surface.

Gold Ore

In every other biome I visited, I could only find gold ore in the bottom 32 layers of the world. Much to my delight, in badlands it was present at all levels. I smelted several stacks of gold ore to make gold ingots, which came in handy for crafting all sorts of equipment.

I used stone buttons to add detail to the exterior.

Rails helped me transport the gold ore around the station.

Cave Spiders

Everything was going well until I discovered that the mine shaft was infested with cave spiders. These poisonous arachnids caused significant damage to my health when they got close enough to bite me. I soon learned to run in the opposite direction if I saw a corridor full of cobwebs – a cave spider spawner couldn't be far away.

DARK FOREST

This dangerous biome was crawling with hostile mobs due to the low light level, created by the dense trees and huge mushrooms. My view was obscured and my movement slowed as I tried to find a path through the gloom, and I nearly fell into a cave opening on more than one occasion. Avoid settling here when you first start out, but consider tracking down a woodland mansion when you're more experienced – they're laden with treasure.

DARK OAK TREE

WOODLAND MANSION

VEX

LARGE OAK TREE

EVOKER

VINDICATOR

HUGE BROWN MUSHROOM

HUGE RED MUSHROOM

ROSE BUSH

OBSERVATIONS

CATEGORY: Medium/lush
TEMPERATURE: 0.7
PRECIPITATION: Rain
VARIANTS: Dark forest hills
DANGEROUS MOBS: 10

Vindicators

These axe-wielding maniacs appeared intent on my destruction as soon as I set foot inside the mansion. Visually they resembled villagers, and I assumed the two were related. When I managed to defeat one it dropped its axe and a single emerald.

Evokers

The evokers were even more deadly than their vindicator cousins. With dark magic at their disposal they summoned a stream of what appeared to be fangs to attack me, as well as a trio of vex mobs. Somehow I managed to defeat one and it dropped an emerald and a totem of undying. According to legend, the totem of undying has the power to bring you back to life in the event of your demise.

Vexes

I was attacked by three of these tiny, ghost-like creatures. I saw them pass through solid blocks with ease. I was able to defeat them with my enchanted looting sword, and they dropped their own weapons.

Woodland Mansion

I'd been struggling to locate a mansion until I paid a visit to my local village. Luckily, a cartographer traded a woodland explorer map for some emeralds, and it showed me exactly where to find the mansion. Glimpsing this rare structure in the gloom of the dark forest was a particularly exciting moment for me. All manner of valuable items were hidden inside, but it was also home to some nasty hostile mobs.

Mansion Loot

Inside the mansion I discovered a cornucopia of food, blocks and items. There were multiple loot chests containing everything from bread to music discs. Interestingly, the rooms containing the most valuable treasures were usually concealed in some way, and I found several rare blocks hidden inside other structures like mounds of obsidian or giant statues. It was all very strange…

WIZARD'S TOWER BUILD

The dark forest biome felt like the ideal spot for a dark wizard's tower build. I sealed myself inside to craft new equipment before moving on to my next location.

I added a jagged design to the very top of the turret.

the exterior with ning netherrack terns.

DESERT

This barren, inhospitable biome was no place to settle. The general lack of water made farming difficult, there were no trees for wood and hardly any passive mobs for food. On a happier note, the desert temple contained some rare treasures and the village supplied me with useful items. When in a desert, consider protecting the villagers from zombies to reduce the risk of them being turned into zombie villagers intent on your destruction.

DESERT WELL

RABBIT

FOSSIL

DESERT TEMPLE

CACTUS

IRON GOLEM

DESERT VILLAGE

VILLAGER

ZOMBIE VILLAGER

HUSK

OBSERVATIONS

CATEGORY: Dry/warm
TEMPERATURE: 2.0
PRECIPITATION: None
VARIANTS: Desert hills, desert lakes
DANGEROUS MOBS: 9

Zombie Villagers

I spotted several zombie villagers in the desert – these unfortunate creatures were once regular villagers but were transformed during zombie attacks. They inflicted damage in the same way as regular zombies, so I stayed out of their way as much as I could.

Fossils

A few blocks below the surface, I found a large fossil. It's rumored that fossils are the remains of ancient creatures, long gone from the Overworld, and they appear to be made from bone blocks.

Desert Village

There were a number of useful blocks in the desert village, from a furnace in the blacksmith's to loot chests and bookshelves in the library. I also raided the farm for wheat, carrots, potatoes and beetroot.

Husks

The desert was crawling with husks. This terrifying zombie variant was somehow immune to sunlight, making it even more of a threat than a regular zombie. It also blended in well with the sand, particularly at night, making it difficult to spot.

Desert Temple

I couldn't see much of interest when I first ventured inside the desert temple. It was only when I mined the terracotta blocks in the floor, and nearly fell through the hole, that I discovered a hidden chamber below. It contained four loot chests, rigged up to several blocks of TNT. Working out how to circumvent the trap mechanics took me a little while, but it was worth the effort.

PYRAMID BUILD

Inspired by the naturally generated desert pyramids, I created a smaller pyramid of my own design, along with a sphinx statue. I used it as a temporary base each time I passed through the desert.

Desert Well

There was a small well built out of sandstone blocks. Since water was in such short supply, this was a welcome sight – it provided me with the water I needed to create a small farm.

The pyramid made a great treasure store.

I built the sphinx just for fun.

Rabbits

The usual grass-loving passive mobs were nowhere to be found in the desert, but I did see lots of golden rabbits. They blended in well with the ground, making them difficult for predators to spot. They were a useful source of food and sometimes dropped the rare rabbit's foot item, which I needed to brew potion of leaping.

Temple Loot

The loot beneath the temple included string, bones, rotten flesh, enchanted golden apples, horse armor and diamonds. In the village blacksmith's, I discovered bread, an enchanted book, gold ingots, iron ingots, obsidian and more diamonds. Not a bad haul for such a barren place.

FOREST

The forest biome was something of a double-edged sword. The abundance of life meant it was a joy to explore during the day. However, when night fell, I found it difficult to navigate around the trees and to spot hostile mobs. Sometimes hostile mobs lurked in the shade and surprised me during the day, too. If you intend to settle in a forest biome, be prepared to undertake quite a bit of tree-felling to make space for building.

RED MUSHROOM

OAK TREE

APPLE

RABBIT

FLOWERS

SUGAR CANE

FALLEN TREE

BIRCH TREE

DUNGEON

BROWN MUSHROOM

OBSERVATIONS

CATEGORY: Medium/lush
TEMPERATURE: 0.7
PRECIPITATION: Rain
VARIANTS: Wooded hills, flower forest, birch forest
DANGEROUS MOBS: 7

Trees

Oak trees dominated the regular forest biome and the birch forest was populated by the distinctive birch tree. Fallen trees were common, too. When mined, oak leaves dropped delicious apples.

Rabbits

There were lots of rabbits hopping around the flower forest. Some had brown fur, others had salt-and-pepper fur and a few were black. I was able to collect plenty of raw rabbit, rabbit hide and rabbit's feet.

Flowers

The flower forest was carpeted in a layer of colorful blooms – it was a very pretty sight. I used them to decorate my house and to dye several of my items.

FOREST CABIN BUILD

With so much wood at my disposal, a rustic cabin seemed the ideal build for the forest. I created a clearing for it to sit in, then enjoyed watching the forest life from the comfort of my new abode.

I used several types of wood to create contrast.

Strategically positioned balconies provided a great view.

Dungeon Loot Chests

The dungeon loot chests contained bread, gunpowder, string, an enchanted book, a saddle and diamond horse armor – a fitting reward for fighting off an army of skeletons!

Dungeon

I was mining a little way below the surface one day when I nearly fell into a hole – I'd discovered a dank, dangerous dungeon! Inside was a monster spawner, spewing out skeletons. I disabled it with torches, then fought off the skeletons before claiming my reward and ransacking the two loot chests.

JUNGLE

The first time I discovered a jungle, I was awestruck by the size of its native trees – some were more than 30 blocks tall! The mysterious temple was a huge draw for me as a loot-seeker, and the biome was teeming with life. The dense foliage made travel difficult and the landscape was quite hilly in places. Falling off cliffs was a risk, but I trod carefully and my efforts were rewarded. Jungles are well worth seeking out once you're more experienced.

FERN

COCOA POD

OCELOT

RABBIT

FLOWERS

MELON

JUNGLE TEMPLE

JUNGLE TREE

OBSERVATIONS

CATEGORY: Medium/lush
TEMPERATURE: 0.95
PRECIPITATION: Rain
VARIANTS: Modified jungle, jungle edge
DANGEROUS MOBS: 7

Parrots

I spotted many of these vividly colored birds fluttering a little way above the ground. I tamed several with seeds and even trained them to sit on my shoulder. They crowded around dangerous mobs, giving me time to escape.

Jungle Temple

It's rumored that this ancient structure was built by early civilizations seeking shelter from the heat and protection from the terrible mobs that spawned in the dark. Its builders clearly owned many valuable items, and I was pleased to discover hoards of treasure hidden inside the temple.

Temple Loot Chests

One of the temple's loot chests was protected by an arrow trap. With my heart pounding, I found a way safely through it. The second chest was hidden from view. I found three levers at the bottom of the stairs and, when I pulled them in the right order, a treasure room opened!

Cocoa Pods

I collected cocoa beans by mining cocoa pods, then used the beans to bake cookies and to dye some of my items a rich, chocolatey brown.

Jungle Trees

These distinctive trees towered over everything around them. They were an abundant source of wood and I spotted cocoa pods growing on their broad trunks.

Melons

Melon blocks were nestled snugly in among the dense foliage – in fact, jungles were the only biome in which I saw melons growing wild. When I mined them, several delicious melon slices dropped. I have heard you can also use them to brew a potion of health.

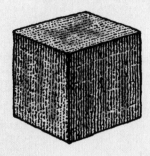

Ocelots

Once I had earned their trust by bribing them with raw fish, these wild felines transformed into loyal friends. Creepers seemed to fear them, so they made great companions as I explored the world, and I made sure to always have one by my side.

TREEHOUSE VILLAGE BUILD

It occurred to me that the jungle's dense tree canopy was big enough to house several builds, and living above the jungle floor would significantly lower the chance of a hostile mob ambush, so I built a treehouse village. Since several dangerous mobs can climb vines and ladders, I made sure to structure the village in such a way that they couldn't be able to ascend.

Walkways between the buildings provided me with easy access.

The swimming pool with a view allowed me to relax and cool off.

MOUNTAINS

As it was easily visible from a distance due to the dramatic mountain ranges and cascading lavafalls, I was struck by the harsh beauty of this highland biome. At first glance it seemed quite barren but, when I looked more closely, I saw rich veins of coal and iron ore running through the stone. There weren't many trees, so avoid mountains if you have a lot of crafting to do. Be careful when exploring cliff edges and enchant your boots with the feather falling effect.

WATERFALL

DIORITE

STRONGHOLD

MONSTER EGG

SILVERFISH

LAVAFALL

LLAMA

GRANITE

EMERALD ORE

ANDESITE

OBSERVATIONS

CATEGORY: Cold
TEMPERATURE: 0.2
PRECIPITATION: Rain and snow
VARIANTS: Gravelly mountains, wooded mountains
DANGEROUS MOBS: 8

Monster Eggs

I knew something wasn't righ[t]
when the stone block I was
mining took longer than usua[l]
to break. This was the only cl[ue]
that all was not as it seemed –
the block in question was, in
fact, a monster egg block with
silverfish inside.

Emerald Ore

While mining beneath
the mountains, I spotted
the bright green glint of
emerald ore among the
stone. What a treat! It
dropped emeralds when
I mined it, which I used
as currency to trade with
nearby villagers.

Silverfish

This repulsive
creature emerged from
the monster egg block, and
I hit it with my sword until it
perished. This seemed to attract
more of them, however. There
were also several silverfish in the
End portal room.

Stronghold

I spent a long time searching for a stronghold, then found one
quite by accident as I was mining beneath the mountains. The
labyrinth of passages eventually led me to an End portal room –
the gateway between the Overworld and the End dimension.
When I filled the empty End portal frames with eyes of
ender, the portal activated, but I wasn't ready to
jump through just yet.

Llamas

A large herd of these strange creatures lived in the mountains.
They seemed to love clambering up the cliffsides, with little
concern for their own safety. I accidentally hit one with my sword
and it spat at me, dealing a fair bit of damage! I was eventually
able to tame them all and equip them with chests to help me
transport my items. They formed a caravan and traveled in a neat
line behind me. Extraordinary!

made use of the
different types of
stone to add variety.

CLIFFSIDE HOUSE BUILD

The mountains were the ideal spot for me to build a cliffside house so I had a safe place from which to enjoy the stunning views. I worked with the landscape and mined into the stone rather than building on top of it.

A multilevel build seemed ideal for this cliff face.

Exposed Stone

The exposed stone of the mountain biome looked bleak at first glance, but I found rich veins of coal ore running through it. I also found the rarer types of stone (andesite, diorite and granite) exposed at surface level and happily mined as much as I could carry.

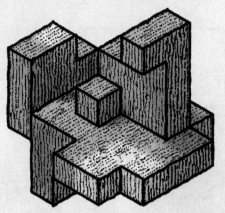

Stronghold Loot Chests

To my delight, I found many loot chests in the stronghold – in storage rooms, in tunnels and in the library, too. I found everything from bread to enchanted books inside.

RED MUSHROOM

BROWN MUSHROOM

HUGE BROWN MUSHROOM

MUSHROOM FIELDS

I sailed a very great distance before I came across this rare biome; it was surrounded by ocean on all sides. The lack of resources made crafting difficult, so I would advise you not to settle here if you're short on supplies. On the other hand, I found it to be very safe due to the absence of hostile mobs, and that made it a particular favorite of mine. Obviously, if you're a mushroom enthusiast, this is the biome for you!

CAVE

HUGE RED MUSHROOM

MYCELIUM

LAKE

FLOATING ISLAND

MOOSHROOM

OBSERVATIONS

CATEGORY: Medium/lush
TEMPERATURE: 0.9
PRECIPITATION: Rain and snow
VARIANTS: None
DANGEROUS MOBS: 0

Mycelium

The ground was covered in mycelium – a curious variant of regular dirt that gave off tiny spores. It provided the perfect environment for mushroom growth, allowing them to flourish at any light level, but I wasn't able to till it into farmland and, frustratingly, it wouldn't support any other form of plant life.

Caves

As with other biomes, I discovered caves and abandoned mine shafts below the surface. I found mining for valuable ores to be relatively safe here since hostile mobs avoided the biome. To my delight, I didn't see a single zombie, skeleton or creeper!

Loot

Disappointingly, I didn't find any loot in the mushroom fields biome. I did find the usual ores below ground, though, and took advantage of being able to mine without the threat of attack.

Huge Mushrooms

Huge brown and red mushrooms seemed to grow here in place of trees. These structures were generally 6-7 blocks tall, but I discovered one that was 14 blocks high! When mined, I found that they sometimes dropped mushrooms. I experimented with turning the huge mushrooms into makeshift shelters, building on top of the brown variety and hollowing out the red version.

Farming

Despite the lack of resources, I was still able to set up a farm. Once I'd made the decision to settle here, I found some dirt in my inventory, tilled it into farmland, then built a crop farm in the usual way.

MUSHROOM VILLAGE BUILD

During this period I created a simple life for myself alongside the gentle mooshrooms. This village became my refuge for those times when I needed a break from the perils of other mob-infested biomes.

I hollowed out some huge red mushrooms and turned them into small buildings.

I built a mushroom farm so that I could make as much mushroom stew as I liked. Delicious!

Mooshrooms

I'd never seen this delightful variety of cow before visiting the mushroom fields, and it seemed to be the biome's only native mob. I found mooshrooms to be an excellent source of several food items: I sheared them for mushrooms (which, oddly, turned them into regular cows), milked them with a bowl for mushroom stew and also milked them with a bucket for milk.

Mushrooms

Mushrooms were the only naturally occurring food source in mushroom fields, but they grew in abundance. I crafted them with a bowl to make mushroom stew, and with cooked rabbit, a carrot, a potato and a bowl to make rabbit stew. I discovered they could also be combined with sugar and a spider eye to make a fermented spider eye – an important potion ingredient.

OCEAN

Wherever I went in the Overworld, I was never too far from the ocean, but I wasn't able to explore this fascinating biome until I brewed potions of water breathing and night vision. The ocean was full of life, but not all of it was friendly – I found the drowned mobs particularly alarming. If you manage to survive your underwater escapades, you'll be rewarded with rare treasures that will make life under the ocean much easier in future.

DROWNED

DOLPHIN

TURTLE

SHIPWRECK

CORAL REEF

BURIED TREASURE CHEST

BUBBLE COLUMN

OCEAN MONUMENT

ELDER GUARDIAN

GUARDIAN

RUINS

OBSERVATIONS

CATEGORY: Aquatic
TEMPERATURE: 0.0-0.5
PRECIPITATION: Rain or snow
VARIANTS: Warm, lukewarm, cold, frozen
DANGEROUS MOBS: 10

Drowned

I found myself constantly fending off attacks from these horrors. Some were armed with tridents – a remarkable throwable weapon that they dropped when I defeated them. The drowned would occasionally drop a nautilus shell, too, which came in handy when I was ready to build a conduit.

Shipwrecks

There were many shipwrecks on the ocean floor – it must have been a particularly dangerous area, or perhaps there was a battle here long ago. I was happy to discover loot chests inside the shipwrecks, and each contained a treasure map.

Turtles

I saw many turtles swimming in the ocean and, after much observation, I discovered that they always returned to the beach where they spawned to lay their eggs. As the babies became adults, they each dropped a scute, which I crafted into a turtle shell. This piece of headgear allowed me to breathe underwater.

Ruins

The ocean floor was littered with ruined buildings – sandstone structures in warm oceans and stone in colder areas. They varied in size and design, but most contained a loot chest, and one of these contained a curious map, which led me to a buried treasure chest.

Ocean Monument

The enormous ocean monument sat at the very bottom of the deepest waters. At the heart of the monument was a treasure chamber, where I discovered eight solid gold blocks encased in dark prismarine. I fought my way past the vicious guardians and elder guardians to claim my prize.

Bubble Columns

These bubbles looked innocent at first, but I soon realized they were produced by dangerous magma blocks. They had the ability to pull me down to the ocean floor, where I was in danger of taking fire damage or drowning.

OCEAN BASE BUILD

I was keen to build myself a safe place underwater, where I could take refuge. I constructed an ocean base, complete with a lookout post, so I could keep an eye on the activity around me.

I constructed much of the base from stone.

The red sand I collected in the badlands biome came in handy for this build.

The Heart Of The Sea

Inside the buried treasure chest was a strange blue item I had never seen before. I couldn't believe my luck – this had to be the fabled heart of the sea! After much experimentation, I realized that I could craft it with nautilus shells to make a conduit.

Conduit

When surrounded by the correct pattern of blocks, the conduit acted like a beacon and provided me with the conduit status effect when I was nearby. This beneficial effect allowed me to breathe underwater, provided me with night vision and increased my mining speed. The conduit also attacked hostile mobs. What a remarkable structure!

PLAINS

This vast expanse of flat, open space was very easy to build in, so it was an ideal biome for me to settle in. I found plenty of water for farming and lots of animals for food. It was also home to a herd of wild horses, one of which I tamed and rode. There weren't many trees, so I had to explore farther afield to stock up on wood. There was no shortage of flowers, and one area of the biome was covered in bright yellow sunflowers.

LAVA POOL

HORSE

RAVINE

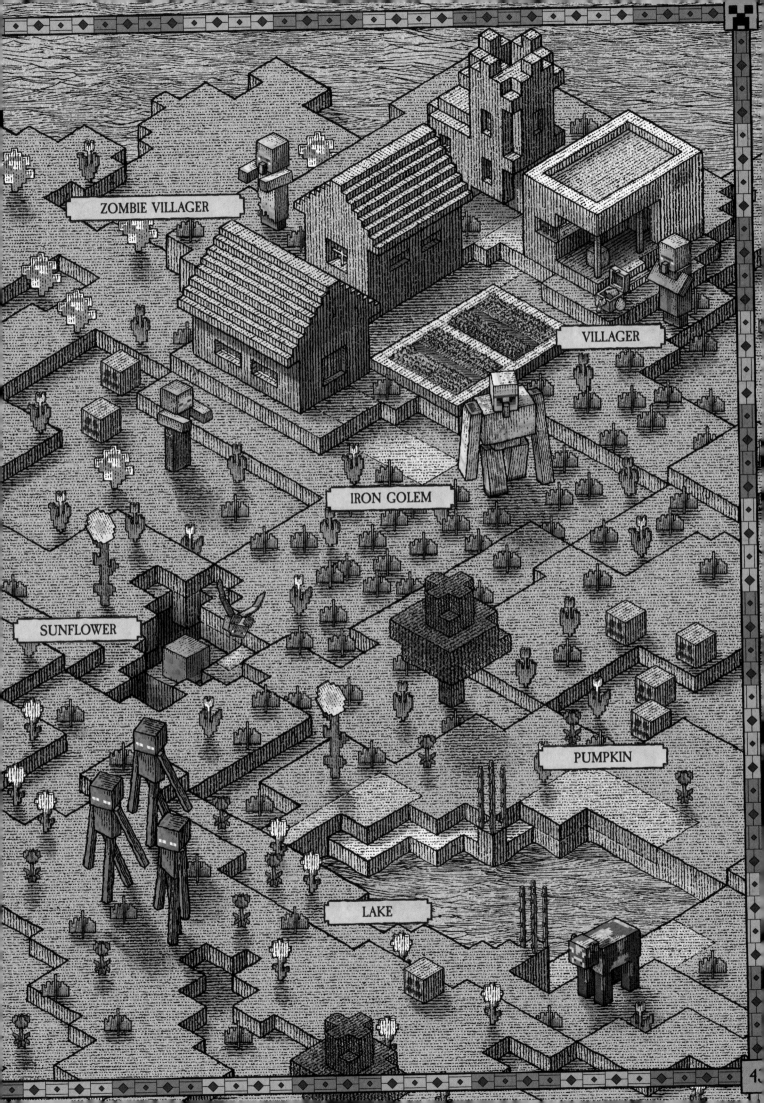

OBSERVATIONS

CATEGORY: Medium/lush
TEMPERATURE: 0.8
PRECIPITATION: Rain
VARIANTS: Sunflower plains
DANGEROUS MOBS: 8

Village

When I arrived in the plains biome, I headed straight for the village. I collected various blocks, traded with the villagers and even took shelter in one of their buildings overnight. Before I moved on, I harvested a few wheat, carrot, potato and beetroot crops from the farm so I could grow my own – I'm sure the villagers didn't mind.

Horses

Plains were one of two biomes in which I found horses. With a little persistence, I managed to tame one and was then able to ride it. My new friend came in handy when I needed to travel long distances, as it significantly increased my travel speed.

Zombie Villagers

I witnessed a zombie attack on the village first-hand, and it was horrifying to watch. I did my best to help, but there were too many zombies and, despite my efforts, several villagers became infected. I'm currently looking into a cure for this dreadful affliction.

Villagers

The villagers were eager to trade with me, and I finally had something they wanted – emeralds! To my delight, several villagers had valuable enchanted items on offer and we quickly came to an agreement.

Village Loot

The plains village I discovered contained another blacksmith's. In the loot chest inside I found obsidian, diamonds, saddles and horse armor.

FARMHOUSE BUILD

Inspired by the simple lifestyle of the villagers, I decided to build myself a farmhouse nearby. I kept the materials simple and constructed it from wood planks and stone.

Sunflowers

A small area of the plains was carpeted in sunflowers, all pointing east toward the sun. On a particularly overcast day, when the sun wasn't visible, I was able to use the sunflowers to work out which way was north.

I enclosed the farm in hedges made from leaf blocks.

I chose a traditional farmhouse style for the roof with overhanging eaves.

Ravine

I saw many ravines as I explored the Overworld, but there was a particularly impressive one in the plains biome. It cut so deep into the terrain that I was able to see rare ore blocks at the bottom, waiting to be mined. As I climbed down, I was careful to avoid the lavafalls and waterfalls cascading down the side, and I kept an eye out for dangerous mobs emerging from caves.

SAVANNA

This arid biome was essentially a vast expanse of dry grass with a small village and the occasional acacia tree. The general lack of water meant crop farming was difficult, but I did see plenty of passive mobs, making it a good source of food. What really drew me to the savanna were the herds of horses and llamas. The peaks in the plateau variant also offered clear views of the surrounding area, which helped me to scout for locations of interest nearby.

FLOATING ISLAND

LLAMA

HORSE

ACACIA TREE

VILLAGE

VILLAGER

ZOMBIE VILLAGER

IRON GOLEM

SUGAR CANE

PUMPKIN

OBSERVATIONS

CATEGORY: Dry/warm
TEMPERATURE: 1.2
PRECIPITATION: None
VARIANTS: Savanna plateau, shattered savanna
DANGEROUS MOBS: 9

Horses

I spent quite a bit of time earning the horses' trust. I was then able to tame several members of the herd and ride them to neighboring biomes.

Village

The savanna villagers had built their village from the native acacia wood, so I spotted the distinctive orange roofs from some distance away.

Food Sources

In addition to the crops in the village farm, I was pleased to find sugar canes growing near water. I spotted the occasional cluster of pumpkins, too.

Llamas

I discovered another herd of llamas in the mountainous area of the savanna – these creatures clearly prefer higher altitudes.

HORSE STABLES BUILD

I got so carried away taming and breeding horses that I soon found myself in need of a stable. I took advantage of the abundance of acacia wood and made sure to craft plenty of hay bales for them to eat.

I separated the horses into individual stalls.

...ated a fenced ...for the horses ...n around in.

Acacia Trees

The savanna was the only biome in which I saw acacia trees growing naturally. Their distinctive orange wood made a great addition to my collection of building blocks.

Flowers

Dandelions and poppies grew freely across the savanna grass. I picked dozens of both and crafted them into dyes, then used them to stain things like glass, leather, concrete powder and beds.

Loot Locations

Never one to miss a looting opportunity, I made sure to raid the chest in the village blacksmith's. Inside I found armor, horse armor, obsidian and diamonds!

SNOWY TUNDRA

The snowy tundra was probably the Overworld's most unforgiving biome, but I made a promise to myself that I would see the dramatic ice spikes at least once. The ground was covered in snow and ice, and trees were rare. Farming was difficult, too, as water usually froze and not many animals spawned here, which made survival more than a little hard. Fortunately, the village and the igloo both contained loot chests for me to raid.

ZOMBIE VILLAGER

ZOMBIE VILLAGE

POLAR BEAR

STRAY

FISH

IGLOO

SILVERFISH

RABBIT

ICE SPIKES

RED MUSHROOM

OBSERVATIONS

CATEGORY: Snowy
TEMPERATURE: 0.0
PRECIPITATION: Snow
VARIANTS: Snowy mountains, ice spikes
DANGEROUS MOBS: 11

Strays

When I saw these creatures shambling toward me, I knew instantly that they were related to skeletons. I only ever saw them in snowy biomes, and they shot arrows tipped with the slowness effect at me as I passed by.

Igloo

As I trekked through the arctic tundra, I spotted an igloo, barely visible against the landscape. It made an ideal emergency shelter as it contained a bed, a furnace and a crafting table. I also discovered a basement below the ground, equipped with a brewing stand, cauldron and loot chest.

Zombie Village

I'd heard rumors about villages that were entirely overrun with zombie villagers, but I'd never seen one before visiting a snowy tundra. The buildings were mossy and covered with cobwebs, and I had to fight off several zombie villagers before I could help myself to the loot.

Ice Spikes

These icy towers only appeared in the ice spikes variant. I climbed a particularly tall one, then hollowed it out and expanded the top to create a base that doubled as a lookout post.

Fish

There were very few sources of meat in the snowy tundra, but I broke the ice on top of the water, got out my fishing rod and managed to catch a few fish.

Loot Chests

There was a loot chest in the village blacksmith's, and another in the igloo basement. The igloo basement chest contained golden apples, wheat and emeralds.

Polar Bears

I saw several of these majestic bears in the snowy tundra, but they were difficult to spot as they blended in so well with the snow. I was always cautious around these animals and made sure I didn't get too close to baby polar bears for fear of angering their parents.

ICE PALACE BUILD

Inspired by the harsh beauty of the ice spikes, I set myself the challenge of constructing an entire ice palace. I used a combination of packed ice, ice and snow, and I still consider it to be one of my finest builds.

The tall turrets gave me an excellent view of the area.

I used wood planks and buttons to create small details.

SWAMP

The swamp was the wettest, gloomiest place I'd ever visited. Much of the ground was submerged in murky water and the foliage was a dull green. I discovered large quantities of clay just below the water and stumbled on a fossil in a cave. I visited this biome for the purpose of tracking down a witch hut, and I found one at the heart of the swamp. I had to fight off a witch and several slimes before I could help myself to its contents, however.

FOSSIL

VINES

LILY PAD

SLIME

HUGE BROWN MUSHROOM

BLUE ORCHID

WITCH HUT

FISH

WITCH

HUGE RED MUSHROOM

55

OBSERVATIONS

CATEGORY: Medium/lush
TEMPERATURE: 0.8
PRECIPITATION: Rain
VARIANTS: Swamp hills
DANGEROUS MOBS: 8

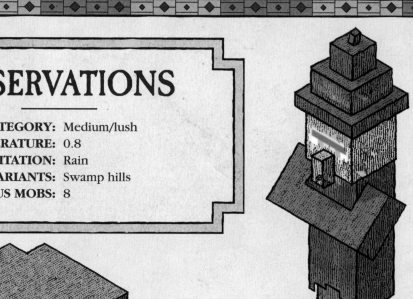

Witch

I encountered a particularly nasty witch in the swamp biome – it pelted me with harmful splash potions, cackling all the while. It was difficult, but I managed to defeat it with my bow and arrows.

Huge Mushrooms

Huge mushrooms sprouted up out of the water, adding to the damp and murky atmosphere.

Oak Trees

The oak trees in the swamp were unlike any I'd seen before. They were covered in vines, and I found them growing in the water as well as on dry land.

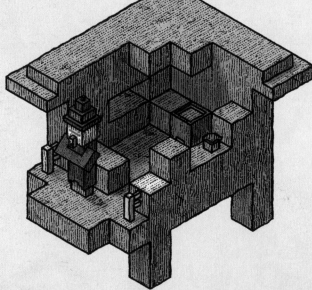

Fossil

I discovered an enormous fossil a little way below the surface of the swamp. After fending off attacks from several slimes, I sealed off the area and lit it up with torches so I could investigate properly. This specimen was even bigger than the fossil I discovered in the desert! I happily mined the bone blocks for use in my builds.

Witch Hut

Although I encountered witches just about everywhere in the Overworld, I only ever saw a witch hut in the swamp. After defeating the witch, I ventured cautiously inside, where I found a cauldron filled with a potion of healing. I quickly helped myself to the potion and the cauldron itself.

HAUNTED WITCH HOUSE BUILD

Inspired by the creepy witch hut, I built a haunted witch house at the edge of the swamp. I made the majority of the house from dark oak planks and constructed a tall tower with a conical roof to give me a view across the water.

I covered the house in vines so that it blended in with the landscape.

The house was built on stilts to raise it above the water.

Blue Orchids

This rare flower grew wild all over the swamp – a bright pop of color in an otherwise gloomy place. I collected several to use for decoration, and to make an attractive light blue dye.

Lily Pads

There was a scattering of lily pads across the surface of the swamp water. I used them as stepping stones instead of building bridges – much more fun!

Slimes

I'd only ever seen slimes in caves before visiting the swamp, but here they squelched across the surface. When I hit them with my sword, they reduced in size twice until they reached their tiniest form. The tiny slimes dropped slimeballs, which I pocketed to make magma cream and sticky pistons.

TAIGA

This cold forest biome had a dense covering of spruce trees, which made it a great source of wood, but dangerous mobs took advantage of the low light level and surprised me during the day. I saw a lot of wild wolves and I was able to tame several with bones. I also discovered strange mossy boulders and a type of soil called podzol in the rare giant tree taiga variant. Keep an eye out for villages tucked between the trees.

PODZOL

MOSS STONE BOULDER

WOLF

IRON GOLEM

FERN

SPRUCE TREE

IGLOO

ZOMBIE VILLAGER

RABBIT

VILLAGER

VILLAGE

OBSERVATIONS

CATEGORY: Cold
TEMPERATURE: 0.25
PRECIPITATION: Rain and snow
VARIANTS: Snowy taiga, giant tree taiga
DANGEROUS MOBS: 9

Loot Locations

I raided the loot chest in the village blacksmith's and found bread, an iron pickaxe, diamonds and obsidian. There was another loot chest in the igloo basement that contained golden apples, wheat and emeralds. Not a bad haul at all!

Podzol

This special kind of soil appeared to support mushroom growth at any light level. Keen to build my own mushroom farm, I mined as much of it as I could carry. Interestingly, I could only collect it if I used a shovel enchanted with silk touch – otherwise it just dropped regular dirt.

Spruce Trees

The spruce trees that dominated the regular taiga and snowy taiga were similar in size to oak trees. The mega spruce trees, on the other hand, were enormous – I only saw these in the giant tree taiga. There was another type of spruce tree in the giant tree taiga biome, which I nicknamed the matchstick spruce since it only had a few leaves at the very top.

Igloo

I almost didn't see the igloo nestled between the trees in the snowy taiga. As in the snowy tundra biome, I used it as an emergency shelter after I got into a scrape with a gang of zombies. Happily, this igloo also had a basement full of useful items, including a brewing stand, a cauldron and a chest.

TREETOP VILLAGE BUILD

The giant spruce trees inspired me to build a treetop village high above the ground. This gave me a stunning view of the landscape around me – at ground level I found it very difficult to see past all the trees.

positioned the village right at the top the tree canopy for e best view.

There was plenty of spruce wood on hand to construct this treetop village.

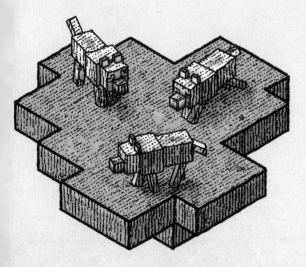

Wolves

Wild wolves roamed the taiga in packs, eyeing me suspiciously. Their thick coats made them well suited to the cold and they seemed to like the cover of the trees. I tamed several with bones and they became loyal companions – they attacked anything that I was fighting, with the exception of creepers. My wolves even teleported to my side when we became separated.

Village

The taiga village was made from spruce wood rather than the usual oak. I made sure to take full advantage of the blacksmith's loot chest and the crop farm as I passed.

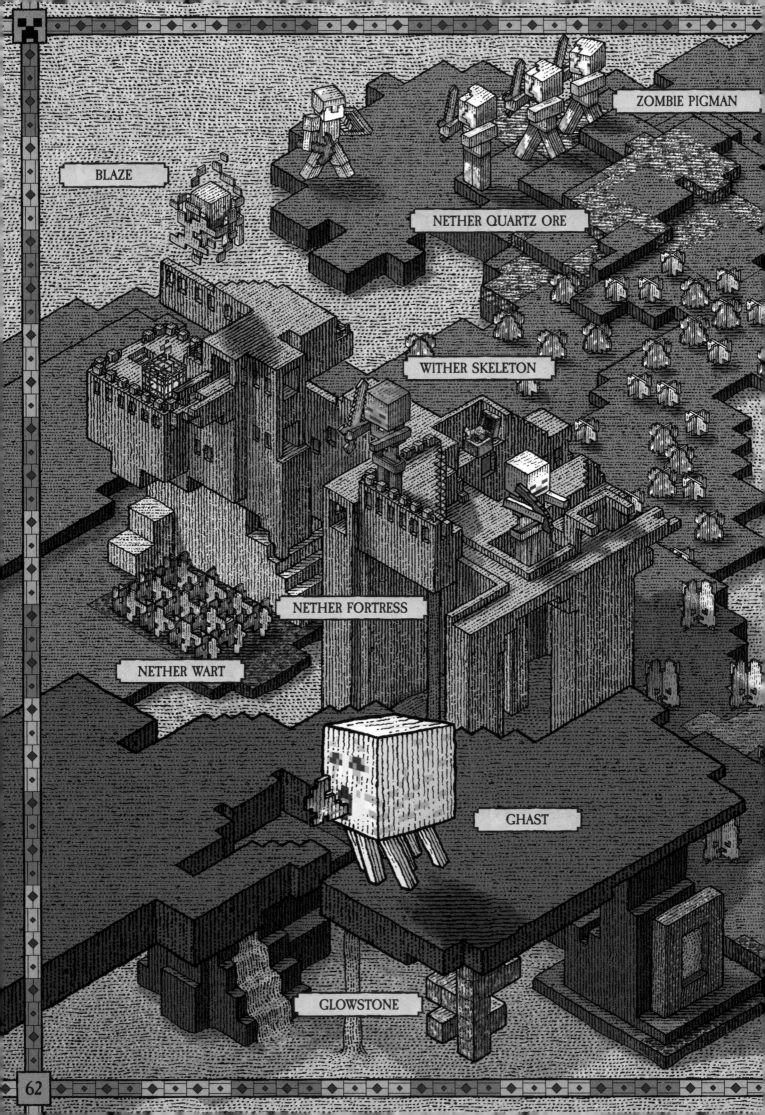

BLAZE

ZOMBIE PIGMAN

NETHER QUARTZ ORE

WITHER SKELETON

NETHER FORTRESS

NETHER WART

GHAST

GLOWSTONE

THE NETHER

The Nether is not technically a biome, but one of Minecraft's three dimensions. I was drawn to the Nether because I wanted to collect the unique and valuable materials found there – in particular, the ingredients I would need to brew potions. Needless to say, it was an extremely dangerous expedition and I was more than a little nervous. I wore a full set of enchanted armor, including items imbued with blast protection and fire protection.

SOUL SAND

NETHERRACK

MAGMA BLOCK

MAGMA CUBE

OBSERVATIONS

CATEGORY: Dry/warm
TEMPERATURE: 2.0
PRECIPITATION: None
VARIANTS: None
DANGEROUS MOBS: 7

Ghast

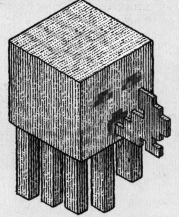

I was horrified to discover this monster could locate me from dozens of blocks away. When attacking, it opened its demonic red eyes and mouth and pelted me with explosive fireballs. I managed to defeat it, and it dropped a ghast tear, which I quickly pocketed – I could use this to make a potion of regeneration later.

Blazes

These flaming mobs emerged from monster spawners in Nether fortresses. They shot fireballs at me and occasionally dropped a single blaze rod when I defeated them. Later, I used these rods to make a brewing stand, and then to make blaze powder to power the stand.

Magma Cubes

Magma cubes bounced around the Nether, leaving trails of flames in their wake. They reminded me of the Overworld's slimes and had the same ability to split into smaller versions of themselves. Big and small magma cubes sometimes dropped a single magma cream, which I could use to brew a potion of fire resistance.

Nether Fortress

The formidable fortress was dark, dangerous and overrun with hostile mobs, but it was also full of treasure. It was built from Nether brick, which I mined to take back to the Overworld for use in my constructions. I discovered several loot chests in the fortress corridors that contained all manner of valuable items. The flint and steel and obsidian were invaluable – I had to use them to repair my Nether portal after it was struck by a ghast fireball!

Glowstone

Blocks of glowstone hung from the Nether ceiling, casting a soft light over the fiery terrain below. I used netherrack to build scaffolding up to the ceiling, mined the glowstone blocks with my shovel and collected the glowstone dust. Afterward, I combined the dust back into blocks of glowstone to create attractive light sources. I also needed glowstone to make redstone lamps.

HELL FORGE BUILD

The Nether struck me as the ideal setting for a dramatic hell forge. The purpose of this build was to provide me with a workstation where I could produce vast quantities of Nether brick. After all, there was no shortage of netherrack to smelt!

I constructed the forge from fireball-resistant stone.

No hell forge would be complete without lava cascading down the walls.

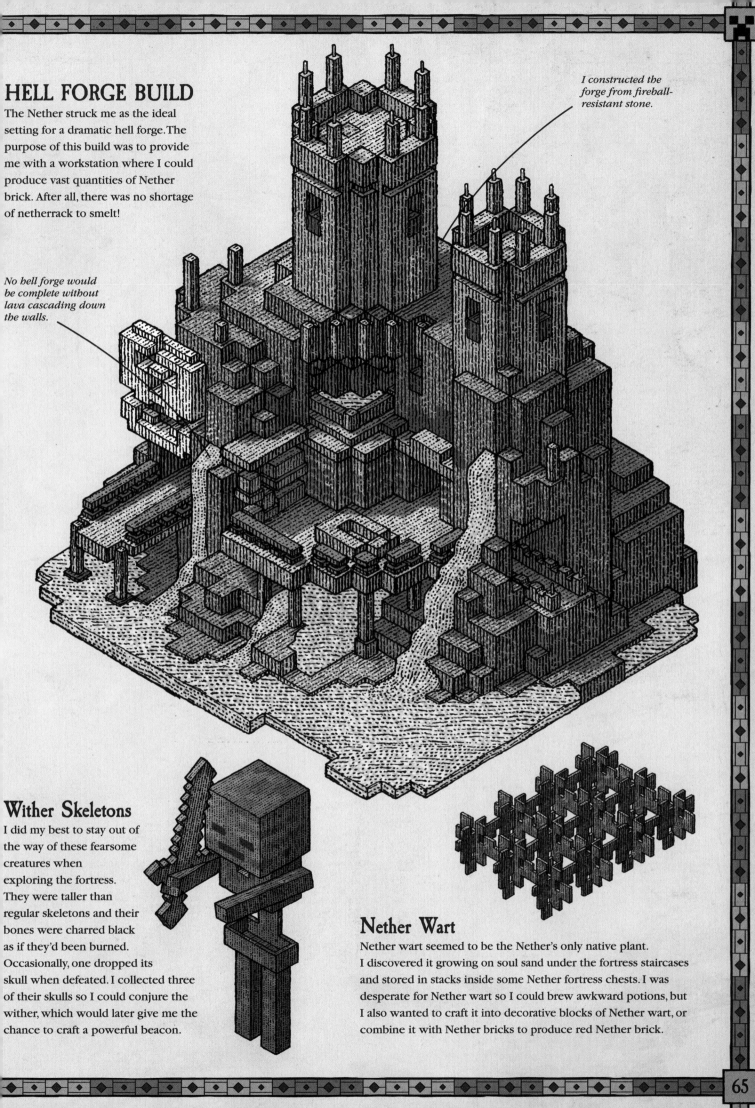

Wither Skeletons

I did my best to stay out of the way of these fearsome creatures when exploring the fortress. They were taller than regular skeletons and their bones were charred black as if they'd been burned. Occasionally, one dropped its skull when defeated. I collected three of their skulls so I could conjure the wither, which would later give me the chance to craft a powerful beacon.

Nether Wart

Nether wart seemed to be the Nether's only native plant. I discovered it growing on soul sand under the fortress staircases and stored in stacks inside some Nether fortress chests. I was desperate for Nether wart so I could brew awkward potions, but I also wanted to craft it into decorative blocks of Nether wart, or combine it with Nether bricks to produce red Nether brick.

THE END

Every loot-seeker dreams of visiting the End dimension – a cluster of barren islands floating in the vast nothingness, known only as The Void. I knew it might be a one-way trip, so it took me awhile to pluck up the courage to jump through the End portal, and I didn't dare visit without my best armor and an inventory full of my most powerful weapons. If you can defeat the ender dragon, you'll find some of Minecraft's most valuable treasures here.

END STONE

END CRYSTAL

ENDER DRAGON

DRAGON EGG

EXIT PORTAL

GATEWAY PORTAL

SHULKER

ELYTRA

END CITY

DRAGON HEAD

CHORUS PLANT

OBSERVATIONS

CATEGORY: Cold
TEMPERATURE: 0.5
PRECIPITATION: None
VARIANTS: None
DANGEROUS MOBS: 3

End City Loot

In addition to several loot chests, I also found elytra in an item frame inside the End city ship. This curious piece of equipment allowed me to glide through the air. At the bow of the End ship, I discovered a dragon head, which many say is a looter's ultimate trophy.

The Ender Dragon

I had to deal with this terrifying beast before I could leave the End with its treasures. I was more scared than I had ever been, but I had a plan. After destroying the End crystals, I shot at the dragon with my enchanted bow and arrows, then hit it with an enchanted sword until it was defeated. Then I claimed my prize – the famous dragon egg was mine at last!

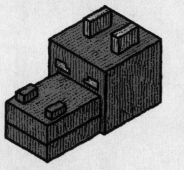

End City

I had to travel across what felt like hundreds of outer islands before I spotted an End city. It was made up of several towers and a floating ship, all of which were built from purpur blocks and End stone bricks.

Portals

As soon as I defeated the dragon, the exit portal activated, giving me the option to travel back to the Overworld. A gateway portal also appeared near the edge of the island. At first I was confused – it was only a block in size and not big enough to jump through. Then it occurred to me to throw an ender pearl through the portal to teleport across.

End Crystals

The dragon drew power from the End Crystals that sat on top of obsidian pillars on the main island, so my first mission was to destroy the crystals. Some were protected by iron bars so I had to mine through those first, which slowed my progress.

DRAGON'S LAIR BUILD

I felt inspired to build a dragon's lair filled with treasure as a tribute to the ender dragon – a truly worthy opponent.

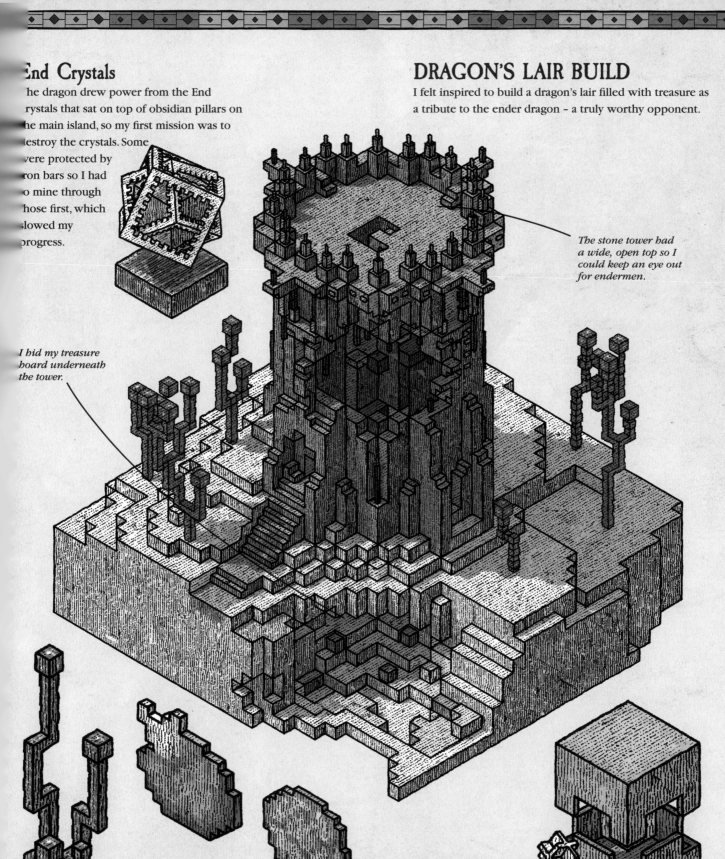

The stone tower had a wide, open top so I could keep an eye out for endermen.

I hid my treasure hoard underneath the tower.

Chorus Plants

These strange plants seemed to be the equivalent of the Overworld's trees. They grew all over the outer islands and, when mined, they dropped chorus fruit, which could be eaten or cooked to make popped chorus fruit. After some experimentation, I realized I could use popped chorus fruit to craft purpur blocks and End rods.

Shulkers

These shell-dwelling creatures attached themselves to the blocks in End cities and shot projectiles at me. The projectiles caused me significant damage and, alarmingly, made me levitate for ten seconds before falling back to the ground and taking further damage. I found shulkers very difficult to spot, too, as they blended in so well with the purpur blocks.

ADVENTURE ACHIEVEMENTS

Now that you're armed with all the information you need to conquer every biome, why not test your survival and exploration skills further? I set myself the following challenges during my adventures – if you're looking to test yourself, you could try them out.

LOOT MUSEUM

Choose a biome you come back to frequently and build a loot museum there. Collect one valuable or rare piece of loot from each biome you visit, then display your finds in the museum.

EXPLORER MAPS

Obtain one of each kind of explorer map – woodland, ocean and buried treasure – and follow them to their respective loot source.

TREASURE STORE

Store your ores as solid blocks in a treasure store. Craft solid blocks of coal, iron, gold, redstone, lapis lazuli, emerald and diamond out of 9 pieces of their respective material.

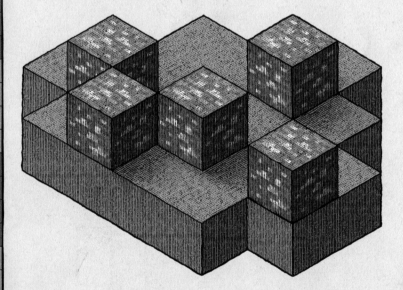

DIAMOND EQUIPMENT

Craft a complete set of diamond armor, plus a diamond sword, pickaxe, shovel, axe and hoe. Only the best will do for an intrepid explorer like you.

FAITHFUL COMPANIONS

Tame a llama, a parrot, a horse, a wolf and a cat to accompany you as you explore. Each of these animals can help you on your adventures.

MINE-CART SYSTEM

Build a mine-cart system that travels between at least two biomes. You can construct a mine-cart station in each biome to store extra mine carts.

SELF-SUFFICIENCY

Build a crop or animal farm in every biome you visit. That way, you'll always have a source of food to fall back on if you run out.

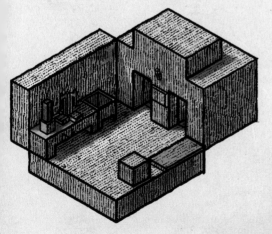

POTIONS MASTER

Create a potions station in one of your bases. Brew a batch of every known potion and keep it stocked at all times so you always have the right potion ready for every adventure.

FAREWELL

Now that I've explored every biome and collected its loot, it's time for me to set off on my next adventure. New biomes, blocks, items and mobs are discovered all the time, so I expect a new opportunity will present itself soon enough.

I do hope that you find my maps and notes useful as you embark on your own quest for loot. Travel safely, and may your inventory be filled with the rarest treasures!

THE LOOTER

STAY IN THE KNOW!

Learn about the latest Minecraft books when you sign up for our newsletter at **ReadMinecraft.com**